Losing the Ring in the River

MARY BURRITT CHRISTIANSEN POETRY SERIES

Hilda Raz, Series Editor

Mary Burritt
Christiansen
Poetry Series

Losing

the Ring in the

River

MARGE SAISER

UNIVERSITY OF NEW MEXICO PRESS

ALBUQUERQUE

© 2013 by the University of New Mexico Press

All rights reserved. Published 2013

Printed in the United States of America

18 17 16 15 14 13   1 2 3 4 5 6

Library of Congress Cataloging-in-Publication Data

Saiser, Marjorie.

  Losing the ring in the river / Marge Saiser.

    pages cm. — (Mary Burritt Christiansen Poetry Series)

    ISBN 978-0-8263-5320-7 (paper : alk. paper) — ISBN 978-0-8263-5321-4 (electronic)

  I. Title.

  PS3569.A4543L67 2013

  811'.54—dc23

                    2012042067

TEXT COMPOSED BY CATHERINE LEONARDO

Composed in Dante MT Std 11.5/13.5

Display type is Dante MT Std

For Don

Contents

III. Liz (1946–)

Acknowledgments

Special thanks to Greg Kosmicki, Lucy Adkins, and Pam Herbert Barger.

I would like to thank the editors of the following journals in which these poems, sometimes under different titles or in slightly different versions, first appeared: "Retina" and "Skinny-dipping with the Neighbor Boys" in *Dos Passos Review*; "The Meal You Bought Me" and "Dancing in My Mother's House" in *Platte Valley Review*; "Mercury in Retrograde" in *burntdistrict*; "Believing Fiction" in *Cimarron Review*; "Before This" in *Chattahoochee Review*; and "Source," "Why I Don't Crush the Spider," and "Wanting to Dance" in *bosque (the magazine)*.

I.
CLARA (1895–1967)

Luke Says It's Another Silly Idea

Me, wanting to show chickens at the fair
and he says I don't have enough

to do, wait until I have babies
to take care of, and of course he's

right. Still, my little banty
struts the yard every inch

a prizewinner, the way he lifts
each foot, places it, the way

his comb shakes and his eye
shines with intention. I could

strut like that, if things were different;
if things were different, I could

strut like that.
Luke says he doesn't know why

I want banties, a pair,
not worth the corn they eat. But I think

maybe there's a place for feathers and strut.
Even a tin can, from the right angle,

glints blue like a diamond in the road.
And the hen lays her eggs

which I boil and have for a second breakfast
when Luke is out of sight. Two of those

like a couple of white stones on a saucer,
my salt, my window, after he's gone,

before I do the dishes. I am
a blue ribbon rascal.

Playing My Cards

The head of the snake sways,
its body coils

in the garden,
its rattles shake out a noise.

I raise my hoe high,
the tongue of the snake

flickers, and I strike.
Down comes my blade

like a judgment.
The jaws of the snake, tailless,

open and close. Something stays me:
its small black eye. The long body

whips in the row of onions,
whips slower, slower. I contemplate

the cards I've been dealt;
the conversation flows on. I see a way

if I can get rid of three losers, just three,
just two,

just this one more trick past the
unsuspecting Luke who

is so intent on winning.
Ah, the jack. That does it. No

stopping me now. Swiftly the
ace, king, queen, and ten.

To all holding cards around this table:
what, exactly, sits here among you,

who, exactly, I will become,
none of us has any idea.

Fight at the Dance

I froze when Luke was knocked down.
The man who had hit him kept his fists up,

ready. The woman they were
fighting about crossed her arms

over her tight white blouse. Luke
rose like a black bear.

The band on the stage kept playing,
but everybody else, even the little kids

who had been shagging around
on the dance floor, stopped. Both men

said all kinds of hell and damn and son-of-a-bitch.
I watched Luke's lips move, the droop and flop of his hair,

the blood run under his nose. I watched his friends
take his arms and steer him

through the door and into the night.
I scrambled in my new shoes to follow after.

Saying I Do

I take a loaf from the oven, cut it, and
the hot slice topples slowly into my hand.

I store salt in a dish in the cupboard
so I can reach in and get a pinch

to sprinkle over eggs in a skillet.
I wash diapers. I wash chore clothes

smelling of pig barn. Every Monday I
clean the clothesline, running a rag over it;

the hand with the rag I raise above my head,
my feet treading the ground.

And that is how I think of myself:
one fist skyward, walking.

I shake the wrinkles out of a wet shirt and hang it.
When it fills like a sail, I run my hand

for a second over its cotton back
before I go on.

I Study Luke

I study Luke while he harnesses the mules;
he says a mule is ugly as a mud fence but
I notice he's soft on them too,
although I've seen him hit Jocko
with a board. Jocko is more

stubborn than Blackie. Luke
caught me between them in the stall, their
muzzles soft as gray velvet,
caught me with half a carrot in each hand,
says he won't let me spoil them. Still I like to
hear the crunch and pop of the carrot,
like to feel Jocko's ears, his warm breath.
Luke admires construction and destruction,

wants whatever is heavy,
whatever resists. When he breaks up
the old foundation,
when he swings the sledgehammer,
his body rejoices,
one shudder per blow.
I watch him hold his bread

and place his mouth on it and bite.
His hair will whiten, outer layer first,
and remain dark underneath
where I'll run my fingers
and grab a handful. I gather
facts about him; I know
the back of his neck,
brown skin with creases,
a mosaic I muse on

when I follow him across the yard
to the barn. His shirt shows
his sweat and when the sweat dries
it leaves a thin white line of salt
in the fabric across his back. This,
I believe, is art.

Wanting to Dance

Move, move, lift my arms
above my head, give my body leave,

corn high money low
the bucket calf loves me.

Move, move,
the beat lives

in my right hip,
my left,

all my easy
easy life. Last night

a breeze swirled the curtains, filled the room.
Move, move all my easy life.

Losing the Ring in the River

Frying eggs in bacon fat
this morning, I think about it.
I don't like to think about it,

the river filling my mouth and throat,
my hands clawing the water,
clawing his arm; he is mad

about that, the scratches on his arm,
and he is mad about the ring,
said he will never buy me another,

said I have a ring if I can find it
on the bottom of the Niobrara.
In part of my mind

I think it was not my fault,
he shouldn't have been holding
my head down and laughing,

but men do that sort of thing. It was
supposed to be fun, cooling off
in the river after a hot day in the field.

Nothing can make him sorry,
not the least bit. I baste the eggs,
blindfolding them the way he likes,

splashing bacon grease over them
with my mother's old spatula. Brown flecks
catch and hold on the yolks. Maybe with time

he'll come to be more loving and kind.

Cause, Effect. Cause, Effect.

I killed a cricket in the house
and after that, everything went wrong.
The corn did not do well,

the dill dried up, the hens choked.
On my hands and knees behind the washtubs,
all I wanted was to

locate the source of the chirp
and subdue it.
I smashed it with a shoe

and as night follows day, Luke
put three sheep into the house yard.
They got to the young pear tree

even though I found a roll of old fencing,
tried to put up a barrier,
tried to protect the soft inner bark.

Cause, effect. Cause, effect.
When I walk home from town Wednesday nights
with the cream check

there is the crunch of my shoes on the gravel
and the white of the beam of my flashlight
reaching as far as it can across the ragweeds.

I Can't Forget

I can't forget how Luke smashed
the hollyhocks, hit the pink and yellow ears
of flowers with his crowbar,
beat on the pump, the porch,

beat the house, stucco
falling off like pieces of crackers.
He leaped down the cellar steps, broke
jars, gallons of pickles and applesauce.
If I could have shut him in, trapped him there,

rolled something heavy onto the cellar door,
and escaped—but he was already
in the kitchen, wrecking flour and sugar,
sweeping plates to the floor;

he beat the mattress, ripped it,
he was roaring. I ran to the living room
where the canary was; Luke
beat the metal of the bed,

he must shiver hands and arms,
he must make old evil hands hurt,
they must be numb.

                    I ran to the road,
the cage bumping my ribs.
Behind me was the noise of an anvil,
hammered, hammered, hammered. I opened
the cage but the canary was afraid,

did not fly. I held it, small, warm, struggling.
I drew out my hand, a bird,
threw it, a fist, into the sky.

This House Isn't Mine

Not the bed, not the pockmarked
pattern of the floor, not

the window I stare from.
Only the ironing is mine.

A clean shirt I raise up
and sprinkle with water from my hand;

the hand is mine, the iron, heating,
that is mine. I take the cuff,

open it and run hot flat metal over it,
nose around the button;

I press along the arms
and leave them flopping, empty,

dangling, while I pay attention to the front and back.
Steam rises to my face, that is mine,

mine the smell of cotton, of penance, of late,
of never catching up, of never quite right.

I hang the shirt on a wire hanger;
the sleeves settle then and keep their

resolution as best they can. I button the front.
This shirt, every thread, is mine.

Why I Don't Crush the Spider

Maybe it's the way all those legs
shuffle and work; maybe
it's the way she makes it

partway up the side of the tub,
slides down. Partway up,
slides down. Maybe it's

because she's in the wrong place
at the wrong time,
doesn't fit in,

doesn't know
shit from shinola,
talks too much

though she's been told *Shut Up.*
I take a clean jar and place it over,
slide a postcard

carefully under. The spider scrambles.
She has no idea
where I lift her to

or what I put her down upon.
It's her job
to wait it out,

the slow blue
then black
of evening. She

doesn't dream of
what she doesn't have,
does she?

In the morning, some of us
get our second chances, get to fling out,
uncaught, into oceans of grass.

When I Have Hurt Him as Much as I Can

When I have fingered the slingshot
lodged for so long in my pocket;

when I have picked up a stone he,
beleaguered, has dropped in passing;

when I have aimed at the white patch of skin
between his pale blue eyes;

when I have pulled back and let loose;
when my stone, sharp-cornered as a word,

sinks in and in,
when its burn equals

some of the wounds I carry,
then as did our mothers and fathers,

he will lie down lonely
and I will lie down lonely,

touching through the blanket.
Distance enough, distance enough.

I Was New and Shiny

When I was new and shiny
and the river was a sister
who liked my least idea,

when winter's sweet cold air
called me out at night
to test the ice along the edges,

I built a fire on the bank
and sat before it,
my old blue coat almost warm enough.

November's fire, November's ground.
I roasted an apple on a fork;
the fruit darkened in the flames,

gave its perfume.
Juice sputtered and fizzed
out the holes in the skin.

The stars held their close
cold mirth
or rather

their tinsel promise.
Some folks will tell you they hear voices, even melodies.
Oh why aren't I what I wanted to be?

My Firstborn, My Eddie, Asks What I Remember

What should I tell him? I began scared
and went to wanting it to be over.

I bit my lip, I screamed, and nobody
helped. The neighbor women tried

to shush me and wash my face. I hit them.
Would hardly stay in bed. One stood

barring the door—I don't blame her now.
Where would I have gone?

I think of it still when I go to clean
that north bedroom or when I use

the sheet with the stain that doesn't
fade. I was unconscious, Eddie,

and didn't feel your weight and heat
laid across my belly,

felt it no more than you remember it,
not even the cry.

You were wrinkled and asleep
when I first held you

and there came a wave
passing across my shoulders and arms.

That's how it was, a wave,
a windless wind

flowing over my body,
telling me how much I would love.

My Daughter, Leaving

Emma stuffed her clothes into a box
and put it into the old Ford Luke
had given her; this was for real.
She shifted into reverse and
started to back up,

then she saw me
standing next to her car and she
stuck her arm out the window.
I grabbed it and kissed her palm,

my old foolish face filling her hand. That's
the kind of thing I think she hates.
We'd had an argument
and after I thought it was over,

we'd started up again. All it takes is
a word or a sigh, a heave-ho
of the body. We were canning
tomatoes, it was midnight,
that's the way we did things. I was filling

jars and she was putting the lids on.
I had to stand there in that steamy kitchen
and take it, dipping those slimy tomatoes
out of the kettle and into the jars,
while she told me every mistake
I ever made. I wanted to fling
hot tomatoes at all the walls. My hands

went on filling jars
and hers went on wiping my spills
off the rims and screwing the lids on.
She screwed those lids very tight,
all the while enumerating.

The smell of the skin of her hand,
the living warmth of it. The car
kept rolling; I took a step to keep up
and then I let go.

Potato Soup

under my knife the peelings drop
into the enamel pan
not quite under my breath I curse him

he is pigheaded and tight
nothing in the gold locket
opening to the strong dark

face foretold I would
run down bugs in a house not
fit for the goat woman

nowhere in the grass the crickets
the stars did it prophesy coal dust

my mother warned
against Irish against strong fingers
chop them into convenient sizes
the potatoes
the onions
she warned he would smell of onions

while it is boiling throw
the peelings to the chickens
wipe my hand on my coat
not even a decent henhouse

milk and butter and salt
float the pepper on the top
turn the gas low at least it's
not cobs

the squeak of the rocker repeats, repeats
the light goes down
on the wall the pattern
of lace and cedar branches
fading

rise

stir

Eddie is dead under this snow

Luke comes from the barn
one more time supper is ready

The First Cicadas

When we were courting
and Luke took me to the Apple Inn,

he said I never did eat more
than soup and salad anyway

so he talked me out of the entrée,
but if I could travel,

I'd eat any number of things. Especially
shrimp. I don't care what he said

about the dirty tail
and the vein and the head. Yesterday

I heard the first cicadas
announce the end.

A few good years left, maybe.
And here is my little dog

waiting on the couch with no light
and here is the dark earth waiting

and birds unseen in the maple,
folded wing and grasping foot.

The sun will start the music; I've
always been lucky.

Today a Dust Devil

Today a dust devil
spirals above the road, finds itself
a shape, spins. Why do I remember
Eddie

          combing his hair:
slick each side, slick the top.
He had to duck to be able to see himself
in the little mirror above the sink.
It was the job

          that killed him, the shaking
of the bulldozer; I couldn't
stop him. Pancakes
for supper,

          a clean shirt,
and he'd stand at the sink and talk
to me. He said he liked to dance at the Playmor
with the Davis girl.

          He'd dip his comb
into the basin and wet his hair.
The dust devil has thinned, has
dropped what it held, motes
falling like a small rain.

          Once, while combing,
he smiled at himself in the mirror
and said he had to get ready
to go see a vixen.

Deciding to Write

Stove whose maw I open and feed
coal I have carried from the shed.

This house Luke thought good enough;
these worn blue flowers of linoleum

I step on. Nothing will stop me. Fat
body in this dress I made

from a pattern I laid piece by piece
onto what cotton I had,

smoothed, pinned, cut, and sewed.
I pull it over my head

and then my old cardigan for warmth.
I build this fire, drop in the last

chunk; I will use up the coal, every crumb.
I take my tablet and pen to the same table

where I cut the garment,
the dress a color not brown.

Let me lay words on paper;
let the grit gather on the floors.

I Tell Myself a Story

The rocker creaks: *Cal-a-*
forn-eye-aye, Cal-a-
forn-eye-aye.

Look, the mighty hen
struts the yard. My children
sit around the table, their faces

bright cups in a row.
My beefsteak tomatoes, sliced,
my green snap peas,

my gravy bowl passed hand to hand.
A fence rings the house.
Red barn. Black-and-white cows

loafing, white bags of breath
above their noses.
I pull weeds, I pick

cucumbers hidden in the shade
of big-heart leaves,
I wash the dirt off my hands

in a bubbling aquifer,
hold water in my palms
and bring it to my face, splash it

cold as aurora borealis
on my neck, my arms.
Eddie, alive and well,

carries a pail of milk to the house,
his earflaps up, jaunty
in his denim jacket, jaunty

in his eight-buckle overshoes.
A brown loaf on the breadboard,
silver spoons in the china cabinet.

In the cellar, applesauce
like nectar in the jars.

II.
EMMA (1925–1996)

Retina

My life moves
on the retina
upside down,

this night in spring,
Arcturus a pinpoint
on the curve of a small black curtain.

If I were anywhere
instead of here on the driveway,
running once more away from home—

if I were at the river,
cranes would land
in the small theater of the retina,

flap in the near-dark,
and find a place to settle.
But here is the image of my mother,

inverted, diminished,
windows of her house behind her,
her shoulders round,

arms hanging,
mouth awry,
cheeks wet.

What will I make of this,
of anything?
The fine black lines

of the feet of the cranes
dance upside down
in the globe of the eye.

She recedes, student of broken things.
For me: the windshield and the dash,
my oncoming implacable road.

Source

We slid down the snow of the riverbank
on a big piece of cardboard,
the cardboard halting at the bottom
and our bodies going on forward
to sprawl on the ice.
Too old for play but we played,

slid on our bellies,
the frozen river under us.
Your hand in your glove
holding my hand in my glove,
we moved further in this world,
found the Day by Day Café, entered,

our glasses fogging over.
We said yes to the soup
and when the young cook
in a long skirt set two
in front of us, the steam
rose, curling over on itself.

Sorcerer, priestess, she
moved her hands above the bowls,
rolling dried herbs between her palms.
This is how it began:
tiny pieces falling
into yours and into mine.

Marriage: Jump Rope

Marriage: multiplication, subtraction
ox pulling a little red wagon
skirt over your head
amber beads on a string, the string
racket of claims
that which I lost and never had
fine print on the label
grunt tussle
firewater ghost of electricity
grave and awkward
no one to tell me
old dog new dog wild dog wolf
damage that was done
the thing itself, the thing itself
mermaid with streaming hair
sun-flooded
shazam
knife to cut an apple with
ticket stub, curtain up
water running under stone
where my mind flies
cocoon unwinding
endless city whose window I lean from
drawing me out of myself
my desolate bed
a bumping into the coffin
theft deception
a gold bell, brown bread.

One Summer Only

We dropped peaches into boiling water
long enough to cook the skins,

then plunged them
into a sink full of ice cubes. The skins

came off when we rubbed them.
You cut the fruit and into each jar

I laid a pit, as I had seen it done.
I don't know why, I said;

must there be a reason?
We set the jars into the canner and left them

while we took a walk in the corn.
It was midnight; we moved

down the row, listening to crickets,
corn between us and on either side, forever.

When I looked at your silhouette,
it was you and corn against the sky,

and corn leaves brushed our bodies
like slender hands.

I Could Have Named It Love

That white apron I tied over my red dress,
those black strappy heels I moved around in,
the crust I filled with apples

and slid into the oven:
I could have named it E for Effort.
I could have named them Good Enough: my young legs

going nowhere
under their skim of skirt.
My fingers curled

around each ear of corn
before the drop
into the steaming pot.

Perhaps it names itself Devotion. I called you
when the meal was ready. You have to admit that. You have to
give me this much: white plates

graced the tabletop,
brown tea floated cubes of ice,
each fork lay in place beside its shiny knife.

Eventually

You wanted a bender
on your own like the old days;
you may have been thinking
Pabst, Bud, chaser,
half a pack of smokes, clean tee shirt,
might rain. I may have been thinking

left like baggage, sauce for the goose,
sauce for the gander. I took the pickup
and drove to Tiny's
where I thought you would

eventually show up.
I parked, sat outside, drove back
in the storm. I didn't make it
up Windmeyer's hill, slid off into the ditch,
and sat thinking in tune with the rain on the roof,

lightning showing the hood
and the cattle at the fence. Eventually
I slogged barefoot in the downpour
toward the farmhouse,
a high heel in each hand.

The Meal You Bought Me

How deep our trouble,
        how odd I felt when
                you ordered nothing, sat

across from me in the silence of the place
        and took pulls on your cigarette. I had my
                mound of mashed potatoes,

cornered oiliness of fish.
        It seemed as if I fingered a
                frayed blanket, tried to

draw it around the shoulders
        of whoever I was:
                a woman so lonely

I didn't want to know her. You and I were
        just beginning to be strangers. Silent meal
                beside the highway. I couldn't decide

where I wanted to look:
        trucks the window held and let go of,
                held and let go of;

square heavy glass of the ashtray;
        your fingers taking the cigarette
                up to and away from your lips.

Labor

My mother picked up a piece of clotted blood,
wiped it from the floor with a Kleenex,
a motion of stooping down and scooping up.
Her purse under her arm, she followed me down the hall
of the small-town hospital

and she probably knew the names of the people
in the chairs in the waiting area, but I didn't.
I knew only the pains of labor
and that I had been there hours and hours
waiting for all this to be over,

no husband holding my hand,
and I walked the hall
because the nurse thought walking might help.
I held my back and held my front,
that hobbling holding groaning posture of motherhood

and motherhood also following it around
whatever hall it's in, mopping up its spill and its trail,
its red stain. The doctor
goes home for Sunday dinner

and motherhood is pain in regular increments.
We've started something here that must be
stayed with, must be traced after in its wobbly circles,
its keening cry followed,
until it can lie carefully and heavily down and deliver.

That Moment When

that moment when I glimpsed
how he really felt, my beloved,
how only his chin showed it,
nothing else, only the bone under the skin

that moment when, laying a trap for myself, talking,
I fell talking into it;
talk had dug the square-cornered
hole and talk had
laid the trunks of young saplings
over the opening and talk had
spread twigs and leaves to cover, to hide,
and talk brought my feet
one, then the other,
and talk made what I walked on
give way

that moment when I almost sat
in the rocking chair
but stopped
and oh god my child was at that moment
crawling from behind the rocking chair
quick as a child does
and her beautiful round perfect head
the nape of it the curve of it
was between
the wood of the china cabinet
and the edge of the back of the rocking chair
so many other times a harmless juxtaposition
but this one time my daughter's head there
—I stopped—something stopped me

the moment when the nail tore
into the thigh of the child
sliding down the roof for fun,
tar paper roof, no place for a child to play

but I played there, I was the child,
the long gentle slope had looked like
a place to slide,
and red blood ran from the tear onto
the black tar paper

the moment when the manta ray
swam in the blue-white water,
its cape-body fluttering around its beak-mouth,
no eyes, no face, the wire of its tail,
black fluttering curtain
coming toward me,
the stranger, the interloper, the weak

the moment the car lurched
and the speedometer went past
90, 95, 100,
and the road came fast toward the windshield,
the curve ahead now already here,
the white truck and the red car behind it
because my foot is on the accelerator pressing down,
pressing down because my husband, my
angry had-enough husband in the passenger seat has
jammed his boot on top my shoe
on top the accelerator

look then at the trees:
they stand in their black trunks
for the gray rain,
the pearls of the drops
striking and striking;
they do not have any other work;
they stand straight for the cold thunder;
they cast their thin arms
to catch the small but rising wind.

Cut and Cut

It was as though I cut and cut
through connective tissue
the way my father
used to skin goats,

his fingers pulling on the flap of hide
to keep it taut for the knife,
to ease it loose from the body,
freeing pelt from meat.

I hacked at what held;
my blade was words: *What*
is
your
problem?

The words you had said to me—
I said them to myself
when I took my walk every morning.
I cut myself free with syllables.

Shiny sharp
jackknife blades
slipping between the hide
and the flesh of the torso,
between the hide
and the muscles of the flank.
Poor little goat. But he was dead already

on old sheets
in the trunk of the car.
His front legs curved,
pretty head bent back,
beard a tuft,
hooves black and precise.
His tail a work of art, a flag
which had been, on better days,
always in motion.

Final Hearing

We—you—repair the light fixture
in our daughter's room. I hold

the candle, and you the screwdriver;
our child sleeps on, dreamless or dreaming,

as we had slept, dreamless or dreaming,
on a soft square in our chamber,

you and I, reaching with our
hands, rolling together

or apart, while the house
failed, as if a spotted

snake moved in the walls,
drawing circles around us.

I hold the candle, you the screwdriver,
the girl sleeps. Thank you,

I say, and blow out the flame.
I don't say: your new alarm clock will be

louder than the old one.
I don't say: I'm sorry

I didn't like the table you bought me.
It seems I should thank you for

catching the gerbil. You pick up
your last suitcase.

Nights Aren't the Worst

Rather it's afternoons; the light from
the window makes too much
of the room, too much of the table, the chair.

Midnight is a smooth shell
to bring to the face, touch to the lip.
The child sleeps, fists curled;

the cicadas' song rises, falls.
You and I stood on the bridge one morning;
it was the summer of the drought,

remember? The river had no water
unless it was hidden
under white sand. Two boys

rode their ATVs
bank to bank, crisscross tracks
where the channel had been.

Coping

Eat too much;
stay up late because the day

has not yielded enough;
no day

ever
yields enough.

Necessity is the floor
we move our chairs around on.

I build it, day after day,
with cracked hands.

Grudges make hallways;
ambition, ceilings.

This is the house that will keep me alive.

Length of the River

I lie crosswise on the bed
so the length of the river
will lie

along the length of my sleeping self.
Strange the things
that give us comfort.

Our ceilings were
flat white skies, our
walls strong as doubt.

What else to do but leave,
locking the house,

folding the key away?
Plaster and curtains and carpet
might have caught what we wished for, sleeping,

might have caught what drifted up in the dark
from our bodies, sparks

from the accidental touch.
I said the river was gray
but at night it runs more silver

and the things humans
gather and store
do not show up much

under the moon;
the good we want to do

moves like a channel
restless
around the fallen trees.

Mercury in Retrograde

In the telescope the sun is a red disk,
red because of the filter, and
a prominence boils out of the corona.
Prominence: those thoughts which fall back

into themselves
and shoot out again. You used to
draw me into the room and close the door
and kiss me and crush me

and there was a day we escaped together, left
the car on the edge of the field.
Smell of alfalfa, drying; sound of
our feet through the hay.
We went toward what we wanted.

In the telescope there is
the sun's flat red cheek
and on it

a dark freckle: Mercury in retrograde,
the dress, unbuttoned, tossed to the ground.

California Moves Farther Away

California moves farther away,
an unreachable coast
shining with fruit,
buildings of pale stone
high heavy bells
dark square windows. Someone once
made me believe the sound of water,
a fountain, a courtyard.

What is real: a long-necked bird
spreading its wings to dry—
not as graceful as I had hoped,
not as sleek. That bird will
be what it is,
its mouth open
and its neck crooked.

The horse in the fog
at the edge of the yard
steps out:
a gray gaunt body. It will raise its head
to stare before it turns back.

Here is my bite of ordinary bread,
my butter on the tongue, my salt.

Love, I'm Done

Love, I'm done with you; Love,
      here's the deal. Last night
            I went to the river. The sun

was barely gone and long strings of cranes
      came from the fields, wavering
            toward me where I stood

on the bridge. Long knotted strings and
      the trilling in all their throats. Love,
            I'm going to pull on my heavy boots,

search my topographical instruments, put my
      fat finger on the map where I intend to
            take myself. May those boots

lead, may they tramp, may they persevere,
      cracked, caked,
            relent never.

I will find a house in the snow—
      open the door—
            thousands of candles!

I Wade In

I wade in,
the river seeping

into the seams of my boots,
my arms empty. When was I

ever prepared? Along the bank,
trees shed leaves like snow.

I am not so sad
as I sound

and maybe you aren't either.
It was only me

being myself
and all my family tree; it was only

all the grandmothers
speaking out of my mouth.

One season becomes another;
I am a thin gold boat on the water.

Raising Liz

Wool does not burn in a flame,
not burn but char.

Changed, not consumed,
I bore down in a brown haze
and pushed her out into the doctor's gloved hand

polished her baby shoes
pulled her nightshirt over her head fed her
carrots rice red jello breaded cutlets bought her a kite
watched her fly it above the park
said happy birthday drove her to class when she was sick
on testing day I did that. Wool does not burn but char.

The beluga circles in a tank at the zoo,
a great tank and very pretty, but a tank,
and in it she circles.

Her hand—for it is a hand—
palms water.

I heard my daughter cry,
opened my eyes in the dark.

Ghost-white beluga in the water.
Bones of a hand
wave toward what lies beyond the glass.

Before This

Before this I was at my daughter's house
she has problems and sometimes
you think she *is* her problems
that's all she is but
I tell you she is more than her problems
and before that I was at home in my sunroom
built with money my mother left me
and before that I had a mother
who wanted me to call her
but I didn't
and before that I was in a bad marriage
as if a marriage is a country
or a neighborhood and you move
and find yourself a better one
and before that I had a slim waist
I had a filigree earbob given by a cheapskate
who told me a long story about how special it was
and before that I believed what anyone told me
and before that I splashed
in the Keya Paha River with my friends
and went home to eat doughnuts
my mother made homemade doughnuts
do you know how good that is?
and before that I was a cream puff my father
stuck his finger into
on Wednesday nights when my mother
went into the town
and before that I was a seed, a lovely seed
like a cottonwood seed,
having my own small fluff for a parachute
floating from a great height
or maybe I was
yes I think I was an oriole's song.

Therapy

I will tell you of the bay window
and of a wasp dragging its body
across the dusty sill, buzzing and dying.
I forget what my mother said when she told me
to play by the window; I remember the cotton doll
with the metal head,
blue eyes that closed when she lay down
as mine were supposed to close when I lay down.
The sun came through the bay window
hot as fever. I put my finger on the doll's eye though
I had been told not to; because I had been told not to,
I didn't push on the eye, though my finger
was just the size to fit through the hole
where her eye lay
staring up at the ceiling,
which she would never have been able to do
without my intervention: I held her eye open,
one of them, and felt the short thick lashes,
the cold blue iris. What did I want her to see?
What would I see now,
and at what cost,
if I opened one eye?
Her forehead did not dent when I
banged her on the windowsill.
I confess this is smoke I'm dragging you through.
I lived like a fish in a bowl
behind that bay window. In that house
I was a good girl.

Let Me Write About Her

Let me write the milk-stink in the rags
she draped every morning to dry;
they hung like thin gray bats
in the porch. Let me say she
carried me one teeth-grit summer,
carried me and a milk pail and
shook off her cow-barn clogs
before she entered the house,
set the pail down,
and made supper. A kuchen
filled with custard,
sprinkled with cinnamon.
Let her break eggs into a green bowl
and beat them with a fork while
I play with a doll at her feet.
Let her shoo flies off my sleeping face.
She falls out of love without noticing;
there is an enameled pan full of
breakfast dishes and there are
a man's shirts in a basket and his overalls
flapping on the clothesline. There is
asparagus in the side yard for two weeks
in spring and then it goes to seed.
There is no dancing on Saturday night
and coleslaw does not make itself. She shouts
at dogs and children who track mud on the linoleum.
She doesn't sing "It's a Long Long Way
to Tipperary." When I sassed her, my teenage face
and shoulders and the way I stood
perhaps reminded her of someone she had loved;
she loved or hated that and she, like me,
couldn't say a word about it.

When I Lie on My Back and Cross My Ankles

I think of her
on her back on her gurney
before the surgery
when a nurse told her
not to cross her legs, to uncross them
and so of course she did.
Such a good girl, my mother,
and good at denial
as I am good at denial.
Nothing was wrong,
the tumor was not stopping her life,
she refused to
have any part of the facts.
She denied so completely
diagnosis and CAT scan;
the specialist's opinion
rolled off her
like beads of water hissing and dancing
on one of her hot skillets.
I was with her in a chamber made by curtains
pulled around her bed;
they would wheel her away soon.
She waited for her turn under the knife,
a phrase she used. What I said was
I have your glasses and your watch, Mom.
She fretted about these things
which touched her all day
or she touched. *I'll see you
on the other side of this,* I said,
standing beside the high white bed
that held her up to me like a hand.
The man who would do the anesthesia
asked her how much she weighed;
he had a clipboard, was writing this down, and I figured
the amount of anesthesia might depend on it
in this emergency surgery. She said 150.

No, not that much, I told him,
she'll say what sounds good, what she thinks you want to hear.
I wanted him to know she twisted facts like pretzels;
the fact was this could have been
the last thing she got from me,
just before a kiss on her too-soft cheek,
the last thing before she rolled away
on her back, legs uncrossed.
My parting shot,
maybe she let that too
roll off.
A nurse raised the low chrome fence between us.
See you after this is over, my mother said,
and she said, *Here goes.*
They glided her away
on the small noiseless wheels
of what she said next. She said: *love you;*
not all
but part,
maybe.

What Do I Want?

My younger brother, carrying old mattresses
out of my dead mother's house,
tosses also a raft of pages

covered in writing. Can you
recall it? I ask him. Anything?
He says he put everything into the fire.

I want what is ash;
I want to be mentioned
in the longhand, the scribble,

like the price of bread,
the lack of rain. She was
crazy at the end, he says.

A cricket sings tonight
here and there around the city,
a set of small black legs in dry grass,

a modicum of body, a serif.
Give me words to fit the tune.
Sing, singer, sing.

Haircut

Pregnant, my daughter stands behind my chair
on newspapers spread on the floor.
She's cutting my hair; I'm crying

because today we've done it again:
that thing about assuming and second-guessing
and saying the wrong thing.

I want to stop this haircut.
Half done is fine with me.
But she keeps cutting.

I grab her wrist behind my head
and we struggle:
one woman sitting on a chair

and another standing behind her,
scissors flashing,
hands grasping.

I let go and sit with my face in a towel;
the blades grate on the hair near my ear,
small pieces no doubt gathering

on the flannel shirt she wears over the baby.
I'm just as stubborn as you, she says,
and more so.

There is the sound
the newspapers make under her feet
as she circles me.

To My Daughter

Feel along the tunnel
and count the openings right and left
in case you need to backtrack. There may

come a spot of breeze
playing around your face, lifting your hair.
Inhale. Take some joy in it

but keep feeling forward with your foot.
Pretend it is I
beside you

or make it someone
you love more.
Your hands will chill,

your palms and your fingers
blind against the wall,
but quitting is colder.

Pretend the dark
is the lake at midnight, no moon.
The sound of air in your throat

is the turning of cottonwoods;
remember how they stir, how they mimic
the sound of surf. Pretend anything that

helps you. Pretend me
out of existence
if it means

you will come sooner into light
at last and see a grassy plain before you,
perhaps one tree,

its arms raised in hallelujah as my arms would
if I saw you,
if I knew you had made it.

III.
LIZ (1946–)

Dancing in My Mother's House

My feet dance on the red rug
my father bought her; she would never
say she wanted but she wanted

and he wanted to please,
besides hadn't the salesman
unfurled rug upon rug

and wouldn't he soon roll them up again?
Buy now Buy now This deal won't last.
I dance as if I had a center, answer

my mother's questions
but do not think of them,
think rather of my hair swaying

with the motion of dancing,
see only walls, framed pictures
sliding by, the stones of the fireplace

they built together, her hands
holding that black stone or that red stone
into place while he chucked white mortar

around it; the sticks of her fingers
wiped the excess away
and everything stayed: stars and planets

in chosen alignment—wait—they slip
out of any semblance of orbit. I dance
because I am bored and because I have feet,

nearly have momentum whirl almost fast enough
my head back with the speed of it
ready so ready *Break away Break away*

Let Me Be the First Snake of Spring

Let me writhe, immodest

Let me be a long white underbelly

Against the warm wrist of the garden

Circle what can be circled

Be hard, be small, be cold

Let me not care

Let the proper wish me away

Let me find their houses

Their stairways in the sun

Their furrows, their lettuces

Let me flick my tongue into the air of

The world which does not love me

Which took my place

Which praises emptiness

Which would step and stomp

With heavy brown boots

Which with any tool at hand

Would be glad

To break the quick coils

Of my beautiful spine.

To the Moon in the Morning

Moon in the morning, chunk of ice melting,
moon wearing no sandals
and half your dress gone, too:

come, breakfast with me;
dance this mimosa down your throat
in my garden of hollyhocks.

No. Don't come. Don't bother. You're like
any other Puritan piece of rock, turning your back
when I show up in a towel

to lie in my hammock. O icy moon of Decency,
never lived on the plains in the summertime,
find your own long-stemmed champagne.

I'll outlast you, Honey,
outlast August and a stinky neighborhood.
Think I'll pay through the nose for my nakedness?

See if I care. Ah but Liebchen,
come closer, warm up. Melt,
you little ice chip, between my heavy breasts.

I Have Nothing to Say About Fire

I have nothing to say about fire
except my father could build one
I saw his hands as he moved logs into place
his hands I would know
anywhere I have nothing to say about hands
except his were old and
good I have nothing to say about good
except that it is connected with lucky

they are right and left hands: *good* and *lucky*
but *good* does not cause *lucky* I could say something about
guilt because my sister on some other side of the world
to the left or right of lucky   .

is biting her lip tasting blood she may be
lying on a blanket thinking of pain
I have nothing to say because I have said it
and am lucky, undeserving, I

who did not earn did not choose did not merit.
I have nothing to say and I have time to say it
and people to listen. I have everything.

Believing Fiction

What I remember is a tale my mother told
about the white dog's death,
about long hair caught under a black tire,
the dog under the car
because it was a spot of shade
while the rest of the county shimmered.
My father, the story goes, hated
having run over the dog. That much
I can believe. He was stricken.
I can believe the Chevy,
the dog's red tongue
curled like the lower petal of an iris,
my father hurrying to go to one of his jobs,
slam of the door, ignition.
The lone shriek. His rush to get out,
his kneeling to look.
The story says he had to finish killing her,
had to get the .22 from the house.
I believe the artifice of the body—
I accept as true
the green tarp he found to carry her,
the weight, the angle of his arms.

Unadorned Fingers, Familiar Palm

When my grandmother lay in her casket,
my father laid his hand on her hand,

inviting me, saying *See, it's all right*
but I shook my head, not wanting to know

if the body is hard, not wanting to know
how cold, how more or less empty.

When my father's body lay in the church
I came early. There was time;

I could have laid my hand on his wrist,
maybe his cuff or his fingers, one cold nail.

I could have straightened
his already straight tie,

but I didn't.
One or another of us, forever

standing before the shell
of what had been,

one or another wanting
and not wanting

one last time to touch. It was my mother
who laid her palm

on my father's hand. My hand
I placed on my mother's back

as I stood with her. I touched
the living, the warm.

Remembering Where I Came From

She had her can of Crisco and there was a jumbo
sack of flour on the table, its mouth open. She scooped
a chunk of Crisco, shook it off the spoon

into the sack. Her strong fingers
worked the flour—whatever it took—
I don't measure, she told me.

Used to use lard, she said. She sprinkled in
some salt, some ice water. Worked again.
She took the lump out of the sack,

put it on the table, took her rolling pin
to it. Eight pies she made that morning
while she talked to me. I peeled the apples. She

crimped the crusts. Pinched them shut to hold
the juices in. *They'll run over in the oven*,
she told me. *They always do.*

I Had Never Seen Anyone Dead

in all my eight years, and I didn't want to—
he had been my uncle, my young uncle,
and I wasn't used to past tense. I was used to
his hands with automotive grime under the nails,

his hand reaching into his pocket to give me
a dime or a quarter for perfection on Friday's
spelling test, his hands prying open a can
of paint, his hands painting my born-

again bicycle blue. I didn't want to go
so I stayed at the house during the service.
My mother said I could help with the babies,
but soon they were napping and there were old women

in charge of them so I washed the dishes. There weren't
many; I washed a jar and its rusty lid,
getting rust on a Sunday-best dish towel.
I tried to wash that out and while I was failing,

my aunt, the bereaved, returned,
her sisters on each side; they went into the bedroom.
I had never heard a grown woman cry, not like that.
It came through the wall.

The next thing would be the meal: the plates, the jello,
white-bread sandwiches, dark brown coffee,
thick-frosted cake. But first there was crying. He had
made the bike new, nearly. He had kept a badger

on a chain; I didn't know how to feel about that:
the badger, flat missile out from under the porch
where it had dug itself a cave, hitting the end
of the chain, being jerked back. I had never seen

sacrifice. The badger did not change,
did not learn, did not domesticate,
did not eat the scraps
my uncle carried to it. The crying

went on. I stood alone
in a kitchen, in my hands
a standard: red-orange stains
on white cotton.

Skinny-dipping with the Neighbor Boys

—using a line by Naomi Shihab Nye

Already I had fractured the rule
about home at sundown

so I stowed my bra inside a cedar,
needles pricking my sweaty skin;

I laid the panties, warm to the hand,
on a branch. I heard

the boys, laughing, cavorting
in the middle of the river.

Fish-belly girl, ready
to wade and to dive,

small-town soul, afraid
but going on anyway,

like everybody,
trying to be what the books say,

holding the head high
but not too high,

stepping out on the particular rocks
we've been given. Give

the fish-belly girl a moment
before the cold current;

give her a moment
under the crescent moon,

her powerful arms out to the night.
There is this, and there is more!

Another Thing I Did Not Tell My Mother

He had a two-door car and good shoulders
under a white tee shirt and he said

he liked poetry and picnics. I forget what
I said. We stopped at Kentucky Fried Chicken and

drove on until we arrived at the bluffs.
We hiked to the top where we could look

down on the river and the trees. It was
Sunday all over the world, chicken

fell off the bone into my mouth, my
fingers were greasy, his too,

and suddenly I thought about
licking the drips off his chin but that was

because his eyes were so open, so blue,
and because it was the last of summer,

the first of autumn. I knew several
poems by heart and he seemed to listen.

We stood side by side above the valley.
All the trees that lined the river

threw their colors at the sky, and the fields
lay flat, cut, shorn. Is this what it takes

years to learn? I could blame it on
the yellow sun and the red trees,

even on the crooked line the river took
across the plain. I turned and he came after,

down into the hundred-year-old oaks
and the shrubs, one bird following another.

Like Everybody

Like everybody's grandfather
my grandfather
kept his fishhooks

pushed through the fabric
of the ceiling of his car,
fishhooks in a row overhead.

I stood on the seat beside him
while he drove,
and I swayed slightly,

barefoot,
a toddler,
the top of my head

not far from the barbs.
Like everybody's grandfather
my grandfather

lay on a bed,
his bed,
his head on a pillow.

He called me.
Some voice will call you,
you in thin thin underwear—

will you have a protector in the house?
A child squatting, looking at
old newspapers stacked under the table.

Looking at newspapers
you can't read—
don't know how.

Some kin
may have
noticed

your lively limbs
your sweet-smelling skin.

You might leave your canopy,
your cave,
if you are lured,

fishhooks near
the unguarded
scalp.

Grow up anyway
and get your own càr.
Get a good one

in a color you like,
as much horsepower
as you can muster,

and drive along the ocean.
Notice

how it lays its palm
again and again
against the white sand

as if to protect.
Pretend
it protects

touches and washes.
Like everybody,
pretend.

Mother and Father Arrive Together in a Dream

My father steps around
to look into her face. You look
so old, he says.
I'm worn out, she says, throwing her head
as a buckskin horse would do.
She sits at my kitchen table
and scoots her chair up. I feel
responsible. I find myself thinking *What if?*
Then, of course, they remember me
and look around. *Just me* I say, stepping
out of shadow. I don't want them to think
I'm hiding anything, keeping anything back.
My mother's hands are in my hair
though I don't want French braids
or any braids at all. I sit
where she had sat, looking at the wall,
waiting it out,
my elbows on the table,
my hands before me. One hand is
hers, and one hand—the dry scaly one—is
his, but the way I hold them,
the way they rub one another,
rolling like water boiling, that
may very well be my own.

My Mother's Bath

In the tub, she guides the cloth
under her floppy breasts, over her white belly,
into the sparse patch between her legs.
I shampoo her hair, my fingers in the foam
over and over her skull,

pour pitchers of water on her
bowed head, wrap her and rub her dry,
thread her arms into the scrap of bra,
hold her steady to step
into panties and jeans. When I pull

the sweatshirt down she emerges, exhausted,
to slump into a chair. Once at a long-ago meal
it was only the two of us
and only tomato soup, but I
went to the breakfront to get two

of the good china bowls and she let me.
Two of the silver spoons. Then she told the
plotless tale about my uncle and the palomino,
changed it to my father, an old story
worth unraveling and putting a new ending on.

I do not let her finish the story of Marion
all over Bob in the back seat after the dance.
I sit on the floor and hold her foot, my fingers
in the towel flicking between her toes.
I do not let her call herself ugly; I flash my

clippers like silver teeth above her yellow
nails and fungus. Nip and cut.
I tell her what I think she told me:
things could be worse, much worse.
I lie any lie I like, her face between my palms.

I say she's my favorite basket case; I say I'll
return come hell or high water.
In her eyes, I see she wants to believe.
I roll my Harley down her drive, gun it,
and send the gravel flying.

Note to My Father After All These Years

Today I spend money. Doodad this, doodad that
in a town in the sun on the border. I sit

outdoors with my doodad dog
at the coffee shop. Time passes.

A man casts a shadow across my latte,
asks if he can borrow my lighter for a minute.

I have none but he talks to me anyway,
generous with conversation,

his tattooed hands giving my dog some
good attention. I can't see his eyes,

only the dark of his sunglasses. His unlit cigarette
bobs in his lips as he talks. This,

or something, reminds me of you. He says
the people here are nice. He loves it here,

says it's way better than the big city; it's all
money anyways; every time he left the house

it was forty bucks. He sees someone
across the street, waves his arm,

shouts: *Jack, I'm free!*
He rises. He's gone.

I Leaned in Close

My mother lay in her hospital bed;
I leaned in close and burrowed my hands
under her back. It was the best hug
we could manage and we managed it.
She was worried about where I would sleep—
that old groove again—and how far
the motel was. Instead of saying something
important and eternal, I said it was nearby;
I said I had my car and she double-checked
all that. She thought I was in danger,
so instead of going
I stayed and we filled a vial of time,
a small glass tube, the way you can carry around
a dram of the Indian Ocean in your purse.
I reaffirmed which light
she wanted left on
and repositioned the nurse call button. I told her
the motel was just down the road
and leaned over her again,
took her bones in my arms
and kissed her face.

Mother, I Wanted

to bring myself perfectly calm
to sit by the gray river.
I wanted to give you what I had accomplished,
what I had worked over, polished, seen clearly, saved.

A pretty string of words like birdsong
to make you love me for a moment.
I wanted to carve a bar of white soap,
to fashion a fish so ideal you would say *Ahhh*.
Its scales I wanted to shape so you would adore me,
so you would think: *This fish can swim*.

I wanted to arrive clear-eyed but last night I couldn't rest;
the curtains in my room I memorized
at midnight and 2 a.m. and 4 a.m.

That thing I promised I would do without fail
I have failed to do.

One of the words you gave me
I placed under a flat cold stone in the garden.

Butterflies came last week to a cottonwood near my house
as you might have known they would.
As you might have known they would,
they clung with their delicate feet
to the surfaces they found.
Butterflies were the new leaves of the tree.
They held there as if it were their plan.
Not one of them could see the whole.

What Belongs to Us Returns Often

The spirit of the house
means no harm
I think; I heard

the soft noise the carpet makes
in that certain spot by my bed.
Later I said

an animal walked
on the rocks outside the window
I had opened

before I went to sleep. (Every day, almost,
I am less afraid.) It means
no harm

but likes to be noticed
as I like to be noticed. *I am
alive; I am here.*

Sometimes at 3 a.m., I make
excuses: the house contracts.
The tiles on the roof

in their unfailing curves
cool under the stars.
A click, a tick

audible through the layers
between us. Those four drops
of water that fall

in the room where
no water is.
Wake me from sleep.

New Love

You fear the river,
its brown blank face.

I, too.

Is it channels
we dread?

Marriage.

That which draws us in or down.
That which has no hesitation.

For our brief season
let us go on side by side

as if creatures with fins.
We keep our round eyes open.

Fear is the watery thing
in which we swim.

You and I, the Cranes, the River

The cranes were silhouettes that night, thousands
lowering in long strings to land in the shallow river.
We stood at peepholes in a shed on the bank,
silent, watching. And I began to wish
someone could see us, witness us,
you and I,
durable in our heavy coats and scarves,
looking out into darkness.
We were not jaded then.
Nothing remarkable happened for an hour,
no talking; we didn't want to spook the cranes
standing on their sandbars, trilling their
all-night song. Then you pointed
toward a peephole in the western wall,
turned my shoulders, mouthed a word,
one word. Vapor rose from your mouth. *Moon,* you said.
We looked at it together, a thin white curved tusk,
a filament, a lost string, a moon on its back.
At a small window we looked at the moon together.

Your Hand Is Injured

We must keep the bandage dry
so I soap you in the tub, your legs and feet,
the soft and yielding dick, the torso,
this body I befriend.
The navel lets go its thimbleful of suds.
My hands wash your hair and wipe your face.
It's March; we've outlasted storms. Any day
the mourning dove returns.
The cottonwood, half-snag,
will keep the place it rooted years ago.
I couldn't get my arms
around it if I tried.
You are napping in the bath, elbow
propping up your wound. Odd embrace
injury gives us. Your hand lowers to my back,
hovers, draws me lightly in.

Take, Eat; This Is My Body

Take, eat; this is my body,
now when you are forming
cell by cell,

small crusts,
the fine chain of your spine.
Lashes, eyelid, brow.

Fingers curling, anthers
of exotic flowers.
Take, eat.

This is a way I love you,
unseen earwig, growing. I will be
blue-white milk at your mouth.

I will be a shadow on a building,
the low sun casting a shape
behind me as I go on.